New England Patriots IQ: The Ultimate Test of True Fandom

Chuck Burgess

2011 Edition
(Volume I)

This title is part of the IQ sports trivia book series, which is a trademark of Black Mesa Publishing, LLC.

Cataloging-in-Publication Data is available from the Library of Congress.

ISBN: 978-0-9837922-6-0
First edition, first printing.

Cover photo courtesy of Scott Horrigan.

Black Mesa Publishing, LLC
Florida
David Horne and Marc CB Maxwell
Black.Mesa.Publishing@gmail.com

www.blackmesabooks.com

New England Patriots IQ

For Dylan, Quinn, Annie,
and Henry ("Hank")

Contents

"We've never really self-proclaimed ourselves anything. If you guys say we're great, we'll accept the compliment."
— Tom Brady, after defeating the Eagles in Super Bowl XXXIX

Introduction

I WAS 14 years old in the summer of 1960 and what a summer it was. My family and I had just moved to a new house in a small town about 20 miles south of Boston called Foxboro (officially spelled Foxbor*ough*).

"Itsy Bitsy Teenie Weenie Yellow Polkadot Bikini" was the number one hit song on the Billboard charts In July and by August Chubby Checker was introducing a new dance called "The Twist."

The summer of 1960 was also the summer that the upstart American Football League came to Boston, represented by a team aptly named "The Patriots."

Up until the arrival of the "Pats," the nearest pro football team to New England had been the distant New York Giants and even as a kid I felt something odd and unsettling about following a team from New York!

So, that fall, when I entered high school and went out for the freshman football team, I had some new football heroes to root for. Instead of following the gridiron exploits of the likes of Frank Gifford, Kyle Rote, and Sam Huff, it was Gino Cappelletti, Butch Songin, and Ron Burton who became my new football idols.

It was a great time to be a kid and a great time to be a Patriots fan.

Now, more than 50 years later I am privileged to write this book about the Patriots, and to still be rooting for the team—now the "New England Patriots"—who call that little town where I went to high school their home too.

From their humble beginning in Boston to their impressive evolution as multiple Super Bowl Champions in Foxboro, the Patriots have provided fans with years of great victories along with heartbreaking defeats, heroes and scapegoats, and thousands of memorable moments from the ridiculous to the sublime.

Along with some editorial comments about the first five decades of Patriots football, two hundred questions about events, facts, statistics, stories, and other tidbits of Patriot football lore are contained in this volume, all of which are sure to test your New England Patriots IQ.

The questions are presented randomly throughout the entire volume, with different degrees of difficulty, and with four possible answers.

Some of the answer choices may look easy, others are sure to pose a challenge, and still others may seem absurd or amusing. Some astute readers may find the answer to one question hidden or referenced to in another question somewhere else in the book, so keep your eyes peeled and your concentration sharp as you enjoy this ultimate test of true Patriots fandom!

Chuck Burgess
August 2011

"We were a team that went on the field and we played. And the AFL was just a great time in our lives. No one had any money. Matter of fact, one time we took off from Boston, stopped off in Buffalo, and picked up the Buffalo Bills on the same plane because we were trying to save money."

— Nick Buoniconti, Hall of Fame Induction Speech

First Quarter—The 1960s

THE BOSTON PATRIOTS were the new kids in town, a football franchise put together on a wing and a prayer by entrepreneur Billy Sullivan and a few of his friends.

The Pats were the eighth and very last franchise awarded by the brand new American Football League and for all ten years of their first decade they struggled for survival—scrimping, struggling, and making due.

Without a stadium to call their own, the nomadic team was forced to play its home games in several different venues from year to year, sometimes within the same season. The Patriots were itinerant laborers within the city, searching for a home and a place to ply their trade.

Yet the red, white, and blue clad team quickly won the hearts of Boston and of New England. Original Patriots Gino Cappelletti, Jim Colclough, Butch Songin, Tom Addison, Ron Burton, Bob Dee and Jim Lee Hunt along with later 1960s stars Don Webb, Jon Morris, Larry Garron, Babe Parilli, Houston Antwine, Jim Nance, Larry Eisenhauer, and Nick Buoniconti are among many legendary players with the team during the early years of the franchise.

The AFL Patriots won 63 games, lost 68, and tied nine from 1960 to 1969 and had three different coaches at the helm. Five of those seasons were winning ones, and five saw the team below .500. The best year was 1964 with ten wins, three losses and one tie. The worst was 1967 when the Pats went 3-10-1.

The American League All-Star Game was the equivalent of today's Pro Bowl Game and it was held from 1961-69. Over the decade the Patriots sent 66 All-Stars to the game, with Houston Antwine making a record six appearances for the Pats.

By the end of the decade, the American Football League was solidly entrenched and the popularity and success of the league forced the senior National Football League to come to terms with the AFL and merge with them.

As the 1960s ended, so did the American Football League, but with its end came one amazing football record that will live forever. Patriots' kicker, wide receiver, and occasional defensive back Gino Cappelletti played in *every* game, in *every* season, of the AFL's existence and finished his career as the top scorer in the history of the league with 1,130 points.

QUESTION 1: During the early years of the franchise the Patriots hosted many preseason games in locations far from their home city of Boston. Where was the very first preseason "home" game played?
   a) Amherst, MA
   b) Manchester, NH
   c) Providence, RI
   d) Worcester, MA

QUESTION 2: Who was the first Boston College player drafted as a number one pick by the Patriots?
   a) Art Graham
   b) Larry Eisenhauer
   c) Dave O'Brien
   d) Jim Whalen

QUESTION 3: Until 1971 the Patriots were without their own stadium and had to play at Boston College, Boston University, Fenway Park, and Harvard Stadium. Which venue was the team's *final* temporary home?
   a) Boston University—Nickerson Field
   b) Boston College—Alumni Stadium
   c) Fenway Park
   d) Harvard Stadium

QUESTION 4: Which year did the Patriots establish a National Football League record of 18 wins (including playoffs) in a single season?
   a) 2001
   b) 2004

c) 2007
d) 2010

QUESTION 5: Between 1960 and 2010 which Patriots player has been selected to the most (nine) AFC All-Star / NFL Pro Bowl teams?
a) Houston Antwine
b) Mike Haynes
c) John Hannah
d) Andre Tippett

QUESTION 6: Which year did the Patriots win their first American Football League or American Football Conference Championship?
a) 1963
b) 1985
c) 1996
d) 2001

QUESTION 7: Who was the first Patriots player elected to the National Football League Hall of Fame?
a) Nick Buoniconti
b) John Hannah
c) Mike Haynes
d) Andre Tippett

QUESTION 8: Who was the first head coach of the Patriots?
a) Mike Holovak
b) Clive Rush
c) Lou Saban
d) Pat Sullivan

QUESTION 9: How was the name "Patriots" chosen as the team name?
a) Suggestion by AFL founder Lamar Hunt
b) Billy Sullivan's daughter picked it

c) By a public naming contest
d) By vote of Boston Public Schools students

QUESTION 10: Which Boston area newspaper cartoonist drew the "Pat Patriot" logo depicting a colonial minuteman wearing a tri-cornered hat and hiking a football?
a) Gordon Stanley
b) Paul Szep
c) Bill Mauldin
d) Phil Bissell

QUESTION 11: The Patriots first permanent home and stadium in Foxboro underwent several name changes during its lifetime. Which of the following was *not* a name for the Patriots first Foxboro home field?
a) Foxboro Stadium
b) Sullivan Stadium
c) Patriots Stadium
d) Schaefer Stadium

QUESTION 12: The Patriots played against a National Football League team for the first time during the 1967 preseason. Which of the following teams was it?
a) Cleveland Browns
b) Baltimore Colts
c) New York Giants
d) Detroit Lions

QUESTION 13: Which Patriots player scored the first *regular season* points in the history of the team and the American Football League?
a) Butch Songin
b) Jimmy Colclough
c) Gino Cappelletti
d) Ron Burton

QUESTION 14: Which of the following players was *not* a first-round draft pick of the Patriots during the 1960s?
a) Jim Nance, Syracuse University
b) Ron Sellars, Florida State
c) Karl Singer, Purdue University
d) Dennis Byrd, North Carolina State

QUESTION 15: The final game played in Foxboro Stadium on January 19, 2001, was in a blinding snowstorm—one of many memorable Patriots "Snow Bowls." Which team did the Patriots defeat that evening in overtime, by a score of 16-13?
a) Buffalo Bills
b) Miami Dolphins
c) Oakland Raiders
d) Pittsburgh Steelers

QUESTION 16: The Patriots were in the first AFL game ever played—an exhibition game played on July 30, 1960. Who did they play?
a) Buffalo Bills
b) Houston Oilers
c) New York Titans
d) Dallas Texans

QUESTION 17: In the legendary "Snow Plow" game at Schaefer Stadium, a lawn tractor equipped with a rotary brush was used to sweep the falling snow off the yard markers. The tractor operator swerved the machine and cleared a kicking spot for Patriots kicker John Smith who made what turned out to be the game winning field goal. What was the brand of that iconic tractor?
a) Ariens
b) Craftsman
c) John Deere
d) Toro

QUESTION 18: The person who drove the tractor that cleared the field in the "Snow Plow" incident above was a work-release inmate from a nearby corrections facility working for the Patriots grounds crew. What was his name?
   a) Mark Hamill
   b) Mark Henderson
   c) Mark Moore
   d) Mark Walhberg

QUESTION 19: The face value for non–luxury box tickets to the 2008 Super Bowl XLII (42) in Phoenix was between $600 and $700 apiece. What was the lowest ticket price for the Patriots first Super Bowl in 1986?
   a) $50
   b) $75
   c) $100
   d) $125

QUESTION 20: Which college coaching position did head coach Dick MacPherson leave to come to the Patriots?
   a) Boston College
   b) Princeton University
   c) Syracuse University
   d) University of Massachusetts

QUESTION 21: Who was the most recent (2008) Patriot player elected to the NFL Hall of Fame?
   a) Bruce Armstrong
   b) Nick Buoniconti
   c) Andre Tippet
   d) Mike Haynes

QUESTION 22: Gillette Stadium was built on the former site of which of the following?
   a) Amusement Park
   b) Car dealership

c) Racetrack
d) State psychiatric hospital

QUESTION 23: Which Boston radio announcing team was the first "Voices" of the Patriots?
a) Fred Cusick and Bob Gallagher
b) Curt Gowdy and Ned Martin
c) Gil Santos and Gino Cappelletti
d) Gil Santos and Bob Starr

QUESTION 24: Which radio station carried the broadcasts of Patriots games in the inaugural 1960 season?
a) 104.1 WBCN-FM
b) 1030 WBZ-AM
c) 590 WEEI -AM
d) 850 WHDH-AM

QUESTION 25: Prior to the official opening and start of the 2002 season, Gillette Stadium was known by another name. What was it?
a) CITI Stadium
b) CMGI Field
c) INVECSO Field
d) TD Place

QUESTION 26: Which Patriots quarterback was also drafted as a catcher by the Montreal Expos baseball team?
a) Tony Eason
b) Tom Brady
c) Matt Millen
d) Mike Taliaferro

QUESTION 27: In 1971, the New England Patriots were briefly known by another name. What was it?
a) Bay State Patriots
b) Boston/Providence Patriots

c) Foxboro Patriots
d) Mass Bay Patriots

QUESTION 28: In which season did the Patriots finally win an overtime game (after ten consecutive losses)?
a) 1975
b) 1988
c) 1994
d) 2000

QUESTION 29: Which of the following Patriots players, while playing for *another* team, returned a punt, returned a kickoff, kicked a field goal, kicked an extra point, and made a tackle all in the same game *against* the Patriots?
a) Deion Branch
b) Wes Welker
c) Doug Flutie
d) Mike Haynes

QUESTION 30: Each time the Patriots score at Gillette Stadium, a group of Revolutionary War re-enactors fire their muskets into the air. What is the name given to these unusual Patriots supporters?
a) Colonial Boys
b) End Zone Militia
c) Patriots Brigade
d) Sideline Soldiers

QUESTION 31: Which Super Bowls did the Patriots play in the New Orleans, Louisiana Superdome?
a) 20 (1986), 38 (2004), and 39 (2005)
b) 31 (1997), 36 (2002), and 38 (2004)
c) 20 (1986), 31 (1997), and 36 (2002)
d) 31 (1997), 36 (2002), and 42 (2008)

QUESTION 32: Which Patriots player set an NFL record by a

lineman for the longest return of a kickoff (71 yards)?
a) Dan Connolly
b) John Hanna
c) Brandon Moore
d) Todd Rucci

QUESTION 33: The Wild Card Patriots upset the Los Angeles Raiders for the Division Championship in the 1985 playoffs in L.A. On the field after the game, Pats general manager Patrick Sullivan got into a verbal, and then physical confrontation with which two Raiders players?
a) Lester Hayes and Howie Long
b) Matt Millen and Howie Long
c) Marc Wilson and Lester Hayes
d) Marc Wilson and Matt Millen

QUESTION 34: When Gillette Stadium opened, what kind of playing surface did it have?
a) AstroTurf II
b) FieldTurf
c) Natural grass
d) SuperTurf

QUESTION 35: From 2001-08, the Patriots often used a defensive player as an eligible offensive receiver when the Patriots were in the "red" zone. That player made five receiving touchdowns for the Patriots during that time. Who was he?
a) Tedy Bruschi
b) Rodney Harrison
c) Richard Seymour
d) Mike Vrabel

QUESTION 36: Who holds the all-time touchdown record for the Patriots from 1960-2010?
a) Gino Cappelletti
b) Sam Cunningham

   c) Stanley Morgan
   d) Randy Moss

QUESTION 37: During the 1960s, the Patriots played in just two playoff games, both in the same season. Which season was it?
   a) 1961-62
   b) 1963-64
   c) 1965-66
   d) 1968-69

QUESTION 38: Gino Cappelletti was part owner of a popular Boston restaurant and nightclub that opened in 1967. What was the name of the establishment?
   a) Daisy Buchanan's
   b) Duke's Place
   c) The End Zone
   d) The Point After

QUESTION 39: Which Patriots player holds the record for the most playoff game appearances (22) from 1990-2010?
   a) Tom Brady
   b) Troy Brown
   c) Tedy Bruschi
   d) Adam Vinatieri

QUESTION 40: The Patriots have always kept an eye on local colleges for talent. Which of these Northeastern University players did the Patriots draft as a number three pick?
   a) Dan Ross, TE
   b) Bob Cappadonna, RB
   c) Chuck Burgess, DB
   d) Jim Murphy, QB

FIRST QUARTER ANSWER KEY

___ **QUESTION 1:** C

___ **QUESTION 2:** A

___ **QUESTION 3:** D

___ **QUESTION 4:** C

___ **QUESTION 5:** C

___ **QUESTION 6:** B

___ **QUESTION 7:** B*

___ **QUESTION 8:** C

___ **QUESTION 9:** C

___ **QUESTION 10:** D

___ **QUESTION 11:** C

___ **QUESTION 12:** B

___ **QUESTION 13:** C

___ **QUESTION 14:** A

___ **QUESTION 15:** C

___ **QUESTION 16:** A

___ **QUESTION 17:** C

___ **QUESTION 18:** B

___ **QUESTION 19:** B

___ **QUESTION 20:** C

___ **QUESTION 21:** C

___ **QUESTION 22:** C

___ **QUESTION 23:** A

___ **QUESTION 24:** C

___ **QUESTION 25:** B

___ **QUESTION 26:** B*

___ **QUESTION 27:** A

___ **QUESTION 28:** B

___ **QUESTION 29:** B*

___ **QUESTION 30:** B

___ **QUESTION 31:** C

___ **QUESTION 32:** A

___ **QUESTION 33:** B

___ **QUESTION 34:** C

___ **QUESTION 35:** D

___ **QUESTION 36:** C

___ **QUESTION 37:** B

___ **QUESTION 38:** D

___ **QUESTION 39:** C

___ **QUESTION 40:** B

KEEP A RUNNING TALLY OF YOUR CORRECT ANSWERS!

Number correct: ___ / 40

Overall correct: ___ / 40

NOTES

#7—Patriots players elected to NFL Hall of Fame: John Hannah, 1991, Mike Haynes, 1997, Nick Buoniconti, 2001, and Andre Tippett, 2008.

#26—The Montreal Expos selected Tom Brady in the 18th-round of the 1995 Major League Baseball draft.

#29—Wes Welker tied an NFL record with his performance as a Miami Dolphin against the Patriots on October 10, 2004 in Foxboro.

"God I love football. And to be inducted into the Hall of Fame is the fulfillment of a lifelong dream. You just don't know what it means to me ... mom and dad would take us to church and as soon as church was over we would fly home to see guys like Ray Nitschke, Gale Sayers, Dick Butkus and all those guys play and man I would sit there and froth at the mouth and say, 'I wonder if I will ever be good enough to play with those guys.'"
— John Hannah, Hall of Fame Induction Speech

Second Quarter—The 1970s

THE SECOND DECADE of Patriots football was one that saw significant changes to the still young franchise. Foremost among them were the American and National Football League merger, the opening of the Patriots first stadium in Foxboro, and the symbolic name change to *The New England Patriots*.

In addition, notorious lawsuits by disgruntled stockholders against the team's management, and a musical chair parade of six different head coaches during the decade, suggested a troubled franchise.

It was also a period of many less-than-stellar teams on the field. In 1970 the team went 2-12, the overtime rule putting an end to the possibility of the many tie games of the past. Two additional 3-11 seasons contributed to a decade that saw just four winning seasons. In the last two years of the decade, the season was expanded to 16 games and the Pats responded on a high note with a positive 11-5 record in 1978 and an above .500 season in 1979, finishing with a 66-78 record for the 144 regular season games of the decade.

Perhaps because of the AFL-NFL merger and also because of the poor performance of many of the teams of the 1970s, the number of All-Star (now Pro Bowl) players dropped to an all-time franchise low of only 15—for the entire decade. Not one Patriots player was named to the Pro Bowl from 1971 to 1975!

Still, Patriots fans found lots of great moments and great players to cheer for. Some were holdovers from the sixties, like Jon Morris, and others would play right into the eighties like John Hannah, Mike Haynes, and Steve Grogan. Other notable players including Bill Lenkaitis, Sam Adams, Leon Gray, Sam Hunt, Russ Francis, Sam Cunningham, Randy Vataha, and Mack Herron gave Foxboro fans plenty of thrills in an otherwise disappointing decade.

QUESTION 41: In the seventh-round of the 1967 draft, the Patriots picked Harvard running back Bobby Leo. What other Harvard player was selected later in that draft?
a) Dave Davis
b) Ray Ilg
c) Bobby Nichols
d) Dick Nocera

QUESTION 42: During the 1970s, the Patriots had two 11-win seasons and made the AFC playoffs only to lose at the end of each of those seasons. When were they?
a) 1975 and 1976
b) 1976 and 1978
c) 1977 and 1978
d) 1978 and 1979

QUESTION 43: Which local automobile dealer and civic leader was instrumental in getting the Patriots to move to Foxboro?
a) Ernie Boch
b) Herb Chambers
c) Peter Fuller
d) Gerry Rodman

QUESTION 44: Prior to the 2011 season, quarterback Drew Bledsoe and offensive center Jon Morris were elected into the New England Patriots Hall of Fame. How many other Patriots had been enshrined in the Patriots Hall of Fame before them?
a) 11
b) 15
c) 19
d) 23

QUESTION 45: Who was the first person nominated to the Patriots Hall of Fame?
a) Nick Buoniconti
b) Gino Cappelletti

c) John Hannah
d) Vito "Babe" Parilli

QUESTION 46: How many Heisman Trophy winners have played for the Patriots?
a) 3
b) 4
c) 5
d) 6

QUESTION 47: What Patriots head coach had the worst winning percentage (.063) in team history?
a) Dick McPherson
b) Phil Bengtson
c) Rod Rust
d) Clive Rush

QUESTION 48: Which of these Patriots head coaches was *not* fired during the season?
a) Lou Saban
b) John Mazur
c) Ron Erhardt
d) Rod Rust

QUESTION 49: Which Patriots head coach has the best opening day game winning percentage (1.000)?
a) Bill Belichick
b) Raymond Berry
c) Pete Carroll
d) Ron Meyer

QUESTION 50: The Patriots defeated Tennessee 17-14 in the divisional playoffs at Gillette Stadium on January 10, 2004. It was the coldest game in team history. In Fahrenheit degrees, what was the official *wind chill* temperature that night?
a) −4
b) −8

c) −10
d) −15

QUESTION 51: In 1960, Patriots president Billy Sullivan asked a local Greater Boston high school cheerleading squad to volunteer as the first cheerleaders for the Patriots. What high school was it?
a) Brookline High School
b) Lexington High School
c) Boston Latin High School
d) Wellesley High School

QUESTION 52: Which of the following kickers did the Patriots acquire as a draft pick?
a) Gino Cappelletti
b) Tony Franklin
c) Stephen Gostkowski
d) David Posey

QUESTION 53: Who was the only Patriots player selected as the MVP of an AFL All-Star Game?
a) Nick Buoniconti
b) Gino Cappelletti
c) Jim Nance
d) Babe Parilli

QUESTION 54: During the early 1960s, without a home field, the Patriots played preseason games against the NY Titans, the Houston Oilers, and the NY Jets at a local high school field. Which of the following Greater Boston schoolboy football stadiums hosted those games?
a) Memorial Stadium, East Boston
b) Cawley Stadium, Lowell
c) Manning Bowl, Lynn
d) White Stadium, Boston

QUESTION 55: During the first five decades of Patriots football, they had the most regular and postseason wins (61) against which of the following opponents?
a) Buffalo Bills
b) Indianapolis/ Baltimore Colts
c) Miami Dolphins
d) NY Jets/ Titans

QUESTION 56: From 1960 to 2010, the Patriots have the most regular season and playoff losses (51) against which of the following opponents?
a) Buffalo Bills
b) Indianapolis/Baltimore Colts
c) Miami Dolphins
d) NY Jets/Titans

QUESTION 57: The 2010 Patriots featured a very talented group of diminutive running backs and receivers—Danny Woodhead, Wes Welker, Deion Branch, and Julian Edelman. What was the quartet sometimes affectionately called?
a) The Brady Bunch
b) The Munchkins
c) The Smurfs
d) The Pee Wee Patriots

QUESTION 58: Between 1960 and 2010, how many Boston College players were number one draft picks of the Patriots?
a) 1
b) 3
c) 4
d) 5

QUESTION 59: A Monday Night Football game on September 21, 1981, in which the Patriots lost to Dallas 34-21, was marred by fan rowdiness and scores of arrests in and around Schaefer Stadium. As a result, the town of Foxboro put a ban on

Monday Night Football at the Stadium. How many seasons did that ban last?

- a) 9
- b) 11
- c) 13
- d) 15

QUESTION 60: On July 30, 1960, in a preseason game against the Buffalo Bills, the Boston Patriots scored the first touchdown in the history of the American Football League. Who was the player that scored that first ever AFL touchdown?

- a) Gino Cappelletti, WR/K
- b) Bob Dee, DE
- c) Ross O'Hanley, DB
- d) Butch Songin, QB

QUESTION 61: What position did the late Francis "Bucko" Kilroy hold with the Patriots?

- a) Special teams coach under the first four Patriots head coaches, 1960-70
- b) Ball boy and later the Patriots equipment manager for over 35 years
- c) General manager and vice president of the Patriots
- d) Schaefer/Sullivan/Foxboro Stadium public address announcer

QUESTION 62: In 1973 the New England Patriots fielded an affiliated minor league team that also played in Schaefer Stadium. What was the name of that team?

- a) New England Minutemen
- b) Massachusetts Militiamen (Mass Militia)
- c) New England Colonials
- d) New England Loyalists

QUESTION 63: The grand opening celebration and first regular season game at Gillette Stadium, September 9, 2002, was a

Monday Night Football game. The Patriots won 30-14. Who was the opponent?
   a) Miami Dolphins
   b) Buffalo Bills
   c) New York Jets
   d) Pittsburgh Steelers

QUESTION 64: Which of these Patriots kickers was known for his unorthodox barefoot kicking style?
   a) Charlie Gogolak
   b) Tony Franklin
   c) Chuck Ramsey
   d) John Smith

QUESTION 65: Which Patriot kicker won his spot on the team via an open public tryout?
   a) Gino Cappelletti
   b) Rex Robinson
   c) John Smith
   d) Joaquin Zendejas

QUESTION 66: Which Patriots backup quarterback jumped to the short-lived New York Stars of the World Football League?
   a) Brian Dowling
   b) Neil Graff
   c) Dick Shiner
   d) Mike Taliaferro

QUESTION 67: What was the seating capacity (to the nearest round number) of Schaefer Stadium when it opened?
   a) 55,000
   b) 60,000
   c) 65,000
   d) 70,000

QUESTION 68: Because of a scheduling conflict with the Red Sox at Fenway Park, a game against the New York Jets in 1968 had to be moved to another site (and out of the state of Massachusetts), *but* was still considered a "home" game for the Patriots. Where did that game take place?

a) Shea Stadium, Long Island, NY
b) The Yale Bowl, New Haven, CN
c) Legion Field, Birmingham, AL
d) Balboa Stadium, San Diego, CA

QUESTION 69: Which Patriots player did ABC television broadcaster Howard Cosell once call an "All World" player?

a) Drew Bledsoe
b) Steve Grogan
c) Russ Francis
d) Jim Plunkett

QUESTION 70: While announcing a Monday Night Football game between the Patriots and the Dolphins, Howard Cosell made a somber and shocking news announcement during the broadcast. What was that announcement?

a) The space shuttle Challenger had exploded
b) President Ronald Reagan had been shot
c) John Lennon had been shot and killed
d) A car bomb had exploded in one of the World Trade Towers

QUESTION 71: In Super Bowl XX (20), the Patriots faced the Chicago Bears who occasionally used massive 382-pound lineman William Perry to carry the ball on short down situations. What was his nickname?

a) The Bus
b) The Compactor
c) The Humvee
d) The Refrigerator

QUESTION 72: Amazingly, Schaefer Stadium took only about one year to be built and was ready for play in 1971. What was the approximate cost of that structure?

a) $3.5 million
b) $7 million
c) $10.5 million
d) $12 million

QUESTION 73: What was the approximate construction cost of Gillette Stadium in 2002?
a) $350 million
b) $400 million
c) $450 million
d) $500 million

QUESTION 74: In keeping with their local roots the Pats have signed many free agents from smaller football programs in New England over the years. Which one of the following was a product of the Division III Tufts University football program?
a) Joe Andruzzi
b) Mark Buben
c) Nick Lowery
d) Bill Nowlin

QUESTION 75: The Patriots won their second Super Bowl over which opponent?
a) Carolina Panthers
b) Chicago Bears
c) Green Bay Packers
d) Philadelphia Eagles

QUESTION 76: Which university did Patriots Hall of Fame wide receiver Stanley Morgan attend?
a) Alabama
b) Kentucky
c) Minnesota
d) Tennessee

QUESTION 77: All-Pro receiver Deion Branch played for the Patriots from 2002-05, and then returned to the Patriots during the 2010 season. How was he re-acquired in 2010?
- a) Picked up off the wavier wire
- b) As a free agent after being let go by the New York Jets
- c) From the Canadian Football league
- d) Traded from the Seattle Seahawks

QUESTION 78: Doug Flutie, Heisman Trophy winning quarterback from Boston College, had a remarkable professional football career playing for New England, Chicago, Buffalo, the New Jersey Generals of the United States Football League, and in the Canadian Football League. How did the Patriots initially acquire Flutie?
- a) First-round draft pick
- b) Trade from Chicago
- c) NFL strike replacement player
- d) Unrestricted free agent

QUESTION 79: When was the last time that the Patriots ended a regular season game in a tie?
- a) 1963
- b) 1967
- c) 1975
- d) 1980

QUESTION 80: What group or individual provided the halftime entertainment during the Patriots first Super Bowl appearance at the Louisiana Superdome in New Orleans?
- a) Wynton Marsalis
- b) B.J. Thomas
- c) Up With People
- d) Combined U.S. Army, Navy, Coast Guard, and Air Force Band

SECOND QUARTER ANSWER KEY

___ **QUESTION 41:** A

___ **QUESTION 42:** B

___ **QUESTION 43:** D

___ **QUESTION 44:** B*

___ **QUESTION 45:** C

___ **QUESTION 46:** C*

___ **QUESTION 47:** C

___ **QUESTION 48:** D

___ **QUESTION 49:** B

___ **QUESTION 50:** C

___ **QUESTION 51:** D*

___ **QUESTION 52:** C

___ **QUESTION 53:** D

___ **QUESTION 54:** B

___ **QUESTION 55:** A

___ **QUESTION 56:** D

___ **QUESTION 57:** C

___ **QUESTION 58:** B*

___ **QUESTION 59:** C*

___ **QUESTION 60:** B*

___ **QUESTION 61:** C

___ **QUESTION 62:** C

___ **QUESTION 63:** D

___ **QUESTION 64:** B

___ **QUESTION 65:** C

___ **QUESTION 66:** A

___ **QUESTION 67:** B

___ **QUESTION 68:** C

___ **QUESTION 69:** C

___ **QUESTION 70:** C

___ **QUESTION 71:** D

___ **QUESTION 72:** B

___ **QUESTION 73:** A

___ **QUESTION 74:** B

___ **QUESTION 75:** A

___ **QUESTION 76:** D

___ **QUESTION 77:** D

___ **QUESTION 78:** C

___ **QUESTION 79:** B

___ **QUESTION 80:** C

KEEP A RUNNING TALLY OF YOUR CORRECT ANSWERS!

Number correct: ___ / 40

Overall correct: ___ / 80

Notes

#44—Players in the Patriots Hall of Fame:
- Gino Cappelletti, 1992
- Nick Buoniconti, 1992
- Bob Dee, 1993
- Jim Lee Hunt, 1993
- Steve Nelson, 1993
- Vito "Babe: Parilli, 1993
- Steve Grogan, 1995
- Andre Tippett, 1999
- Mike Haynes, 1994
- Bruce Armstrong, 2001
- Stanley Morgan, 2007
- Ben Coates, 2008
- Jim Nance, 2009
- Drew Bledsoe, 2011
- Jon Morris, 2011
- Patriots founder William H. "Billy" Sullivan was also inducted as a non-playing member in 2009

#46—Patriots who won the Heisman Trophy:
- Joe Bellino
- John Huarte
- Doug Flutie
- Jim Plunkett
- Vinnie Testaverde

#51—First Patriots Cheerleaders—the Wellesley High School cheered for the Pats because Patriots founder Billy Sullivan lived in the town. The WHS faculty advisor to the cheerleaders was Charlie Burgess, father of the author. As a youngster, the author occasionally joined his dad and the cheerleaders on the Patriots sidelines in 1960.

#58—Patriots all-time number one draft picks from Boston
　　College:
- Damien Woody, 1999
- Jack Concannon, 1964
- Art Graham, 1963

#59—MNF ban in Foxboro, 1982-94.

#60—First TD in the AFL. Defensive end Bob Dee recovered a
　　fumble and scored the AFL's first touchdown.

"We had two Hall of Fame quarterbacks in our division in Jim Kelly and Dan Marino, and he completely changed the passing attack of those two teams. Once he joined the team, the New England Patriots improved dramatically. And he was someone that other people followed and made everyone better."
— Robert Kraft, on Hall of Famer Andre Tippett

Third Quarter—The 1980s

THE PATRIOTS ENTERED the 1980s by rededicating and renaming their stadium. Overall they also rededicated themselves to winning football as well, going .500 or better eight times and eventually getting back into the playoffs.

The worst season for the Pats came in 1981 when they won only two games, but they rebounded by 1985 and 1986 when they went 11-5 both years. However the successes were later marred by reports and then confirmation of substance abuse violations by a number of well-known players.

Despite the drug abuse controversy, the quality of play and the team improved and the number of Patriots named as Pro Bowl players from 1980 to 1990 jumped to 39.

Steve Grogan was again the premiere quarterback of the Patriots during the decade and John Hannah, Julius Adams, and Steve Nelson, holdovers from the 1970s teams, made the Patriots a better club in the mid-80s. Players like Mosi Tatupu, Stanley Morgan, Raymond Clayborn, Craig James, Fred Marion, Andre Tippett, Irving Fryar, and Roland James are a few other notable Patriots of the decade.

QUESTION 81: When did Patriots owner Robert Kraft purchase the team?
   a) 1992
   b) 1994
   c) 1997
   d) 2000

QUESTION 82: Besides the Patriots and the Miami Dolphins, what other NFL team has gone undefeated in regular season play?
   a) Chicago Bears
   b) Dallas Cowboys
   c) Green Bay Packers
   d) New York Giants

QUESTION 83: New England won its fourth AFC Championship on a snow cover field at Gillette Stadium on January 18, 2004, and advanced to Super Bowl XXXVIII (38) by defeating which of these teams?
  a) Carolina Panthers
  b) Indianapolis Colts
  c) Miami Dolphins
  d) Pittsburg Steelers

QUESTION 84: What is the name of the annual award presented by the Patriots in honor of the late Ron Burton?
  a) Ron Burton Media Award
  b) Ron Burton Sportsmanship Award
  c) Ron Burton Community Service Award
  d) Ron Burton Rookie of the Year Award

QUESTION 85: Tom Brady set an NFL and franchise record for the most touchdown passes in a season in 2007. How many touchdown passes did he throw?
  a) 45
  b) 47
  c) 50
  d) 58

QUESTION 86: During the 2007 season, wide receiver Randy Moss also set an NFL and franchise record for most touchdown receptions. How many touchdown receptions did he make?
  a) 30
  b) 23
  c) 18
  d) 13

QUESTION 87: Which Patriots special teams player set the NFL record for the longest kickoff return (108 yards) during the historic 2007 regular season?
  a) Laurence Maroney
  b) Asante Samuel

c) Donte Stallworth
d) Ellis Hobbs

QUESTION 88: Which of the following Patriots players set an all-time rushing record during the 1982 season with 1,385 career yards?
a) Sam Cunningham
b) Tony Collins
c) Kevin Faulk
d) Jim Nance

QUESTION 89: Which Patriots player set an all-time leading receiver record in 2007 based upon number of catches (557) made?
a) Troy Brown
b) Deion Branch
c) Randy Moss
d) Wes Welker

QUESTION 90: As of 2010, who holds the all-time Patriots receiving record of 10,352 yards—nearly 4,000 yards more that the next closest receiver?
a) Troy Brown
b) Irving Fryar
c) Terry Glenn
d) Stanley Morgan

QUESTION 91: Before securing the land to build a facility in Foxboro, Massachusetts, where did owner Billy Sullivan hope to build a stadium for the team?
a) East Hartford, CN
b) Pawtucket, RI
c) Worcester, MA
d) South Boston, MA

QUESTION 92: The Patriots have had several outstanding players from the U.S. Naval Academy on the roster since 1965.

Which of the following Midshipman below played for the Patriots most recently?
- a) Joe Bellino
- b) Kyle Eckle
- c) Bob Kuberski
- d) Max Lane

QUESTION 93: Which former Patriot standout became the co-owner of the Boston Breakers of the United States Football League?
- a) Tim Fox
- b) Bill Lenkaitis
- c) John Smith
- d) Randy Vataha

QUESTION 94: In 2009 the Patriots played their first regular season game outside of the United States. What foreign city was it played in?
- a) Alberta
- b) Madrid
- c) London
- d) Paris

QUESTION 95: Outside Linebacker Stephen Neal was a NCAA wrestling champion. Which other Patriots player was also a college wrestling champion?
- a) Vince Wilfork
- b) Julius Adams
- c) Jim Nance
- d) Andre Tippet

QUESTION 96: Prior to buying the New England Patriots, what connection did present owner Robert Kraft have with the team?
- a) Fan and president of the booster club
- b) Supplied paper products to Foxboro Stadium

c) Owned Foxboro Stadium
d) Director of player personnel

QUESTION 97: Which of the following Patriot kickers did *not* wear jersey number one?
a) Tony Franklin
b) Nick Lowery
c) Eric Schubert
d) John Smith

QUESTION 98: The Patriots have played four preseason games in three different foreign cities during their first 50 years as a franchise. In which of the following international cities were the games played?
a) Havana, Toronto, and Ottawa
b) Mexico City, Toronto, and Montreal
c) Montreal, Vancouver, and Beijing
d) Toronto, Calgary, and Montreal

QUESTION 99: What was the nickname of Patriots all-time great defenseman Ray Hamilton?
a) The Duke
b) Hambone
c) Hog
d) Sugar Bear

QUESTION 100: What popular Patriots running back became an original member of the USFL Breakers?
a) Craig James
b) Andy Johnson
c) Stephen Starring
d) Mosi Tatupu

QUESTION 101: Which former Patriots player had a role in the movie *The Longest Yard* starring Burt Reynolds?
a) Gino Cappelletti
b) Don Hasselbeck

    c) Joe Kapp
    d) Jim Plunkett

QUESTION 102: Which of the original NFL teams have the Patriots played against the *fewest* (eight) times up until 2010 during the regular season?
    a) Chicago Bears
    b) Washington Redskins
    c) New York Giants
    d) San Francisco 49ers

QUESTION 103: Which of the original NFL teams below have the Patriots faced the *most* times (11) up until 2010 during the regular season?
    a) Philadelphia Eagles
    b) New York Giants
    c) Green Bay Packers
    d) Detroit Lions

QUESTION 104: How many head coaches of the Patriots have been named Coach of the Year?
    a) 0
    b) 1
    c) 2
    d) 3

QUESTION 105: What Patriots player was named AFL Player of the Year (MVP) in 1964?
    a) Ron Burton
    b) Gino Cappelletti
    c) Larry Garron
    d) Babe Parilli

QUESTION 106: During the 1960 preseason, the Patriots played preseason games in four different New England cities or towns. Which New England city or town was *not* one of them?

a) Amherst, MA
b) Hartford, CN
c) Providence, RI
d) Worcester, MA

QUESTION 107: After several years of holding training camp at the University of Massachusetts in Amherst, where did the Patriots move their preseason camp?
a) Boston College
b) Bryant College
c) University of New Hampshire
d) Brown University

QUESTION 108: Which of these Patriot players was named the Super Bowl MVP while playing for another team?
a) Nick Buoniconti
b) Tony Eason
c) Joe Kapp
d) Jim Plunkett

QUESTION 109: From 1996 to 2003 the Patriots won ten overtime games while losing only four. How many of those victories were won by an Adam Vinatieri field goal?
a) 7
b) 8
c) 9
d) 10

QUESTION 110: During the 14-game stretch of overtime games the Patriots participated in from 1996 to 2003, the team set an NFL record for consecutive wins. How many overtime games in a row did the team win?
a) 6
b) 7
c) 8
d) 9

QUESTION 111: In 1978, the Patriots went 11-5, hosting and losing the only playoff game ever held at Schaefer Stadium. Who was their opponent?
  a) Cincinnati Bengals
  b) Houston Oilers
  c) Miami Dolphins
  d) New York Jets

QUESTION 112: After Tom Brady, which Patriot quarterback holds the record for most (182) career touchdown passes?
  a) Steve Grogan
  b) Drew Bledsoe
  c) Jim Plunkett
  d) Babe Parilli

QUESTION 113: Which Patriot quarterback holds the record for most (208) career interceptions thrown?
  a) Tom Brady
  b) Drew Bledsoe
  c) Tony Eason
  d) Steve Grogan

QUESTION 114: Super Bowl XXXVIII (38) in 2004 pitted the Pats against the Carolina Panthers. Who was the featured halftime performer(s)?
  a) Aerosmith
  b) Beyonce
  c) Toby Keith and Willie Nelson
  d) Janet Jackson

QUESTION 115: Which of the following punters did the Patriots acquire as a fifth-round draft pick instead of as a trade?
  a) Mike Patrick
  b) Zoltan Mesko
  c) Tom Tupa
  d) Jeff Feagles

QUESTION 116: When did Robert Kraft gain full ownership of Foxboro Stadium?
- a) 2000
- b) 1995
- c) 1993
- d) 1990

QUESTION 117: How was the construction of Gillette Stadium financed?
- a) Public stock options
- b) Municipal bonds
- c) Private investment
- d) Public-private joint venture

QUESTION 118: Quarterback Brian Dowling (1972-73) went to which Ivy League school?
- a) Harvard
- b) Brown
- c) Yale
- d) Dartmouth

QUESTION 119: Which NFL Hall of Fame player was drafted in the fifth-round by the Patriots in 1961, but never played for the Pats and went to the rival NFL instead?
- a) Bob Lilly
- b) Fran Tarkington
- c) Mike Ditka
- d) Herb Adderly

QUESTION 120: Excluding Tom Brady, which of the following Patriots quarterbacks has made the most (131) starts for the Pats?
- a) Drew Bledsoe
- b) Tony Eason
- c) Steve Grogan
- d) Babe Parilli

THIRD QUARTER ANSWER KEY

___ **QUESTION 81:** B

___ **QUESTION 82:** A

___ **QUESTION 83:** B

___ **QUESTION 84:** C

___ **QUESTION 85:** C

___ **QUESTION 86:** B

___ **QUESTION 87:** D

___ **QUESTION 88:** A

___ **QUESTION 89:** A

___ **QUESTION 90:** D

___ **QUESTION 91:** D

___ **QUESTION 92:** B

___ **QUESTION 93:** D

___ **QUESTION 94:** C*

___ **QUESTION 95:** C

___ **QUESTION 96:** C

___ **QUESTION 97:** B

___ **QUESTION 98:** B

___ **QUESTION 99:** D

___ **QUESTION 100:** C

___ **QUESTION 101:** C

___ **QUESTION 102:** B

___ **QUESTION 103:** A

___ **QUESTION 104:** C*

___ **QUESTION 105:** B

___ **QUESTION 106:** B

___ **QUESTION 107:** B

___ **QUESTION 108:** D

___ **QUESTION 109:** C

___ **QUESTION 110:** C

___ **QUESTION 111:** B

___ **QUESTION 112:** A

___ **QUESTION 113:** D

___ **QUESTION 114:** D

___ **QUESTION 115:** B

___ **QUESTION 116:** C

___ **QUESTION 117:** C

___ **QUESTION 118:** C

___ **QUESTION 119:** B

___ **QUESTION 120:** C

KEEP A RUNNING TALLY OF YOUR CORRECT ANSWERS!

Number correct: __ / 40

Overall correct: __ / 120

NOTES

#94—Before a crowd of 84,000 at Wembly Stadium.

#104—Coach of the Year, Mike Holovak, 1966; Bill Belichick, 2003, 2007, and 2010.

"I watched him come into the league and helped him to do the things that he has done. When you find somebody you believe in, somebody who can help you win, somebody who cares about winning as much as you do, then it's your job to help him do his job. I took that personally."
— Bruce Armstrong, on his relationship with Drew Bledsoe

Fourth Quarter—The 1990s

THE 1990S SAW another name change and another re-dedication of the stadium in Foxboro. Four head coaches paced the sidelines, Bill Parcells being one of the most newsworthy and controversial, and the ownership of the team was changed more than once—for better or worse sometimes—but eventually much for the better.

The Pro Football Hall of Fame in Canton, Ohio inducted the first Patriots player and a quarterback who would lead the Patriots toward the twenty-first century, made his debut.

The Patriots got a new look as they updated their traditional red, white, and blue uniforms. Their look changed but their overall record for the decade was still disappointing, only 68 wins in 160 games from 1990 to 1999.

The decade started with the worst Patriot season ever, one win and 15 losses. They improved to 10-6 in 1994 and by 1996 compiled 11 wins and five losses. During the 1990s, 26 Patriots were named to the Pro Bowl.

Defensive tackle Bruce Armstrong was the single player who played for the Pats throughout the entire decade—from 1987 to 2000. Some of the most recognizable Patriots of the era beside Armstrong and quarterback Drew Bledsoe included Ty Law, Curtis Martin, Dave Meggett, Chris Slade, Ben Coates, Troy Brown who made his debut in 1993, and Adam Vinatieri who joined the Pats in 1996.

QUESTION 121: Which of the following quarterbacks, all with less than 15 starts as a Patriot, made the most career appearances (53) for New England?
   a) Doug Flutie
   b) Joe Kapp
   c) Vinny Testaverde
   d) Scott Zolak

QUESTION 122: From the 1963 to 2007 seasons, New England has appeared in seven league championship games. Which of

the following venues was *not* a site for one of those seven championship games the Patriots participated in?
   a)   Alltel Stadium, Jacksonville
   b)   The Astrodome, Houston
   c)   Balboa Stadium, San Diego
   d)   Louisiana Superdome, New Orleans

QUESTION 123: Besides Bill Belichick, which Patriots coach has the most (three) postseason wins?
   a)   Ron Meyer
   b)   Bill Parcells
   c)   Raymond Berry
   d)   Pete Carroll

QUESTION 124: Robert Kraft purchased the Patriots in 1994. Since then, how many years have the Patriots made the playoffs in the 17 years of Kraft ownership?
   a)   9
   b)   10
   c)   12
   d)   14

QUESTION 125: On December 3, 2010, the New England Patriots became the first NFL team to sign a player from the United Football League. Who was that UFL player?
   a)   Matt Gutierrez, QB
   b)   Cory Ivy, RB
   c)   Eric Moore, DE
   d)   Jerry Miller, K

QUESTION 126: Prior to his injury in 2008, how many consecutive seasons did Tom Brady start in all 16 regular games?
   a)   5
   b)   6
   c)   7
   d)   8

QUESTION 127: In which year did New England quarterbacks Steve Grogan, Tony Eason, Marc Wilson, and Doug Flutie all make at least three starts during the regular season?
  a) 1986
  b) 1987
  c) 1989
  d) 1992

QUESTION 128: Which Patriots coach nearly got electrocuted at a press conference when he touched an ungrounded or faultily wired microphone?
  a) Phil Bengtson
  b) John Mazur
  c) Ron Myers
  d) Clive Rush

QUESTION 129: In 1959 Patriots founder Billy Sullivan had to borrow $17,000 from several other investors in order to come up with the AFL franchise entry fee. How much was the entire entry fee?
  a) $20,000
  b) $25,000
  c) $30,000
  d) $35,000

QUESTION 130: In 1969, a player who had just been cut from the Patriots was in the stands watching the game. The public address announcer called his name and he was told to report to the Patriots locker room. A half hour later he was in uniform and made the tackle on the opening kickoff. Who was that player?
  a) Bob Cappadonna
  b) Barry Gallup
  c) Bob Gladieux
  d) Carl Garrett

QUESTION 131: What strange event occurred at BU's Nickerson Field deciding the outcome of a 1961 game against the Dallas Texans, when the Patriots were trying to hold on to a slim 28-21 lead at the end of the game?

    a) The Patriots ball boy tripped a Dallas runner as he ran down the sidelines

    b) A "streaker" ran naked through the end zone distracting the Dallas quarterback who tried to throw the ball at him

    c) A Patriots fan ran onto the field, in front of a Dallas receiver, deflected a pass, and then quickly ran back into the stands

    d) A large dog ran onto the field, tripping up a Dallas runner who probably would have scored a touchdown

QUESTION 132: What city was rumored to be the possible new home for the Patriots when James Orthwein took ownership of the team in 1992?

    a) Cleveland

    b) Hartford

    c) St. Louis

    d) Phoenix

QUESTION 133: Which Patriots opponent added to the Super Bowl pregame "hype" by recording and releasing a rap record called "The Super Bowl Shuffle"?

    a) Chicago Bears

    b) Green Bay Packers

    c) Philadelphia Eagles

    d) St. Louis Rams

QUESTION 134: The Patriots have won many memorable "Snow Games" in Foxboro, undefeated for 11 such games at home during the regular season and the playoffs through the 2010 season. On October 18, 2009, an early New England storm saw the Pats plow under (59-0) which of the following teams?

a) Miami Dolphins
b) Tennessee Titans
c) Indianapolis Colts
d) Oakland Raiders

QUESTION 135: Freezing temperatures seem to be to the liking of the Patriots. They are 24-6 when the temperature at kickoff is 32 degrees or below since 1993. What opponent have they defeated the most times (five) in freezing weather?
a) Buffalo Bills
b) Indianapolis Colts
c) Miami Dolphins
d) New York Jets

QUESTION 136: What Super Bowl opponent of New England was billed as "The Greatest Show on Turf"?
a) Chicago Bears
b) Philadelphia Eagles
c) Green Bay Packers
d) St. Louis Rams

QUESTION 137: Which New England kickoff return man holds the record for most kickoff returns (three) for touchdowns in a season?
a) Alan Carter, 1975
b) Raymond Clayborn, 1977
c) Kevin Faulk, 2000
d) David Meggett, 1995

QUESTION 138: New England holds the NFL record for most touchdowns in a single season scoring 75. Which season did the Patriots score the record 75 TDs?
a) 2000
b) 2004
c) 2005
d) 2007

QUESTION 139: Don Calhoun had a record 5.59 yards per carry average in 1976. Which Patriots runner broke that record in 2010 with a 5.64-yard average?
   a) BenJarvus Green-Ellis
   b) Kevin Faulk
   c) Sammy Morris
   d) Danny Woodhead

QUESTION 140: When the Patriots were "homeless" from 1960-70, one of their rented venues allowed them the use of just one locker room, forcing the Pats to dress at a nearby hotel and meet under the stands at halftime. Which stadium was it?
   a) BC-Alumni Stadium
   b) BU-Nickerson Field
   c) Fenway Park
   d) Harvard Stadium

QUESTION 141: In which stadium was there a fire in the wooden stands forcing Patriots fans onto the field for safety?
   a) BC
   b) BU
   c) Fenway Park
   d) Harvard

QUESTION 142: What is the official seating capacity of Gillette Stadium?
   a) 60,756
   b) 65,756
   c) 68,756
   d) 69,756

QUESTION 143: Which Patriots coach once said, "If they want you to cook the dinner, at least they ought to let you shop for the groceries," alluding to his lack of final approval in selecting players?
   a) Bill Belichick
   b) Pete Carroll

c) Bill Parcells
d) Rod Rust

QUESTION 144: In the 1976 Divisional Championship game at Oakland, the Patriots were "robbed" of victory because of a controversial roughing the passer call by referee Ben Dreith late in the game. The call was so controversial that Dreith was never assigned to another New England game. Who was the penalty called on?
a) Julius Adams
b) Mike Haynes
c) Ray Hamilton
d) Tony McGee

QUESTION 145: In another Oakland game, this time in the 1978 preseason, Patriots star wide receiver Darryl Stingley was tragically paralyzed after he took a then legal but vicious hit from an Oakland defensive back nicknamed "the Assassin." Who was that player?
a) Lester Hayes
b) Ted Hendricks
c) John Matuszak
d) Jack Tatum

QUESTION 146: When the Patriots take the field at Gillette Stadium prior to kickoff, which of the following is blasted over the PA system?
a) "1812 Overture" by the Boston Pops Orchestra
b) "Rock and Roll Part Two" by Gary Glitter
c) "Ride of the Valkyries" by the London Symphony Orchestra
d) "Crazy Train" by Ozzie Ozborne

QUESTION 147: Schaefer Stadium opened on August 15, 1971. The Pats defeated the New York Giants 20-14 in the preseason match before a sellout crowd of 60,423 fans. Who scored the

first points in that contest, the first points ever scored in
Schaefer Stadium?

a) Pete Gogolak
b) Fran Tarkenton
c) Gino Cappelletti
d) Charlie Gogolak

QUESTION 148: The NFL players went on strike in 1982. How
many regular season home games were played in Schaefer
Stadium that year?

a) 3
b) 4
c) 5
d) 6

QUESTION 149: During the second NFL Players Association
strike in 1987, the owners cancelled the games for week three
of the season and then fielded teams of replacement players
until the strike was over. The replacement team games
counted as official games in the year-end standings. What was
the record of the New England replacement team?

a) 0-3
b) 1-2
c) 2-1
d) 3-0

QUESTION 150: Who was *not* a first-round draft pick during
the 1970s?

a) Russ Francis, Oregon
b) Mike Haney, Arizona State
c) Julius Adams, Texas Southern
d) Rick Sanford, South Carolina

QUESTION 151: Team owner Robert Kraft signed an agreement
in 1998 to move the Patriots out of Foxboro. Where was he
going to move the team?

a) Hartford
b) Nashua
c) Providence
d) St. Louis

QUESTION 152: Since it opened, Gillette Stadium has hosted a number of other sports events in addition to New England Patriots football games. As of 2011, which of the following sporting events has *not* been held at Gillette?
a) NCAA Lacrosse
b) FIFA Men's World Cup Soccer
c) High School Football Championships
d) NCAA Football

QUESTION 153: The Patriots have retired seven numbers of former players, all of whom are in the Patriots Hall of Fame. Which player enshrined in the Patriots Hall of Fame does not yet have his number retired?
a) Bruce Armstrong #78
b) Nick Buoniconti #85
c) Gino Cappelletti #20
d) Mike Haynes #40

QUESTION 154: A unique feature of Gillette Stadium is the stylized lighthouse and bridge at one end of the field. The lighthouse is symbolic of the many lighthouses that dot the shorelines of the New England states. Which famous New England landmark was the Gillette Stadium bridge modeled after?
a) Bourne Bridge, Cape Cod
b) Longfellow Bridge, Boston and Cambridge
c) Quechee Gorge Bridge, Vermont
d) Zakim Bridge, Boston

QUESTION 155: Which Patriots head coach frequently used the expression "It is what it is" in his often brief and terse post

game press conferences?
  a) Bill Belichick
  b) Raymond Berry
  c) Pete Carroll
  d) Bill Parcells

QUESTION 156: Which New England kicker booted a game winning field goal in the final seconds of the final home game of the 1978 season, to give the Pats their first divisional title since the AFL-NFL merger?
  a) Jim Baker
  b) Nick Lowery
  c) David Posey
  d) John Smith

QUESTION 157: Frenzied New England fans celebrating the 1985 late season Monday night playoff-clinching victory over Cincinnati tore down the Sullivan Stadium goal posts and carried them down the middle of US Route One. What happened to those goal post pilfering fans?
  a) Several suffered serious head injuries and broken bones as they were hit by the falling crossbar
  b) They were arrested and handcuffed to the goalposts by the State Police
  c) Many suffered electrical burns as the metal posts struck the highways overhead power lines
  d) MNF announcer Howard Cosell chastised them on national television as "churlish, infantile, and moronic fools..."

QUESTION 158: "Patriots Way" is an inspirational film about the Patriots rise to power in the NFL shown in *The Hall at Patriots Place*. Who is the narrator of the film?
  a) Avery Brooks—"Captain Sisko" on *Star Trek: The Next Generation*
  b) Tom Doyle—WROR-FM radio announcer and voice-over actor

c) James Earl Jones—"Darth Vader" in *Star Wars*
d) Gil Santos—the "Voice of the New England Patriots"

QUESTION 159: The Sullivan family put their business Stadium Management Trust and Sullivan Stadium itself up as collateral for a musical tour that Chuck Sullivan co-produced. Exorbitant losses from that venture eventually led to the end of the "Sullivan era" of the Patriots. What was the name of the tour?
a) The Beatles' "Reunion Tour"
b) The Jacksons' "Victory Tour"
c) Madonna's "Like A Virgin Tour"
d) The Rolling Stones' "Steel Wheels Tour"

QUESTION 160: Who was the author of *The Education of a Coach*, a biography of New England coach Bill Belichick?
a) Karen Guregian
b) David Halberstam
c) Michael Holley
d) Bob Ryan

Fourth Quarter Answer Key

___ **Question 121:** D

___ **Question 122:** B

___ **Question 123:** C

___ **Question 124:** C

___ **Question 125:** C

___ **Question 126:** B

___ **Question 127:** C

___ **Question 128:** D

___ **Question 129:** B

___ **Question 130:** C

___ **Question 131:** C

___ **Question 132:** C

___ **Question 133:** A

___ **Question 134:** B

___ **Question 135:** D

___ **Question 136:** D

___ **Question 137:** B

___ **Question 138:** D

___ **Question 139:** D

___ **Question 140:** D

___ **Question 141:** A

___ **Question 142:** C

___ **Question 143:** C

___ **Question 144:** C

___ **Question 145:** D

___ **Question 146:** D

___ **Question 147:** C

___ **Question 148:** B

___ **Question 149:** C

___ **Question 150:** C

___ **Question 151:** A

___ **Question 152:** B

___ **Question 153:** B

___ **Question 154:** B

___ **Question 155:** A

___ **Question 156:** C

___ **Question 157:** C

___ **Question 158:** A

___ **Question 159:** B

___ **Question 160:** B

Keep a running tally of your correct answers!

Number correct: ___ / 40

Overall correct: ___ / 160

"Sometimes in life you've got to get through certain things and there are tough obstacles to overcome — and this was one in my life."
— Tedy Bruschi, on winning Comeback Player of the Year honors after a stroke nearly ended his career

Overtime—The 2000s

THE FIRST DECADE of the twenty-first century was the most amazing period in the history of the Patriots football club. And the performance of the Patriots may have been the most remarkable in the history of professional football.

Forty years after the franchise first took the field in Boston a new era of *championship* football began in New England with ingredients that included a new stadium, a new coach (the only coach for the entire decade), new players, and new attitudes.

Only the first season of the decade witnessed a regular season record of less than .500 (5-11). From 2001 on, the Patriots posted nothing but winning seasons, the *worst* being 9-7 in 2002! In 160 regular season games played from 2000-09, the Patriots won 112 while losing only 48. (The playoff records were similarly impressive, but we don't want to give too much away!)

Interestingly, at the very start of the decade no Patriots players were named to the 2000 Pro Bowl, but from 2001 to 2010, the Patriots sent 42 players to the Pro Bowl and in 2007 a franchise record tying eight were selected.

Quarterback Tom Brady made his first start with the Patriots in 2000, holdover kicker Adam Vinatieri made record setting contributions to the team as did his able successor Stephen Gostkowski, and Tedy Bruschi personified the Patriots with his "never give up" attitude. Matt Light, Kevin Faulk, Richard Seymour, Lawyer Milloy, Larry Izzo, Willie McGinest, Mike Vrabel, Troy Brown, Ty Warren, Ty Law, Vince Wilfork, Wes Welker, Randy Moss, and Rodney Harrison are but just a few of the many, many outstanding Patriots players who come to mind when thinking of the decade.

It was the most amazing era of all time for the fans of New England professional sports. The Patriots played in four Super Bowls from 2002 to 2008 and won three—2002, and back-to-back wins in 2004 and 2005! The Red Sox won their first World Series Championship in 86 years in 2004 and repeated as champions again in 2007. The Celtics rebuilt themselves as an NBA power and won their 17th World Championship in 2008, while the Bruins capped off the decade of Boston and New England dominance by winning the 2010-11 Stanley Cup Championship for the first time in 38 years.

It was a great time to be a New England fan.

QUESTION 161: Which of the following Patriots players landed an acting role in the movies *Dead Heat* starring James Coburn and *Never Too Late*, starring Connie Stevens, Paul Ford and Maureen O'Sullivan?
  a) Gino Cappelletti
  b) Joe Kapp
  c) Jim Nance
  d) Jim Plunkett

QUESTION 162: Many superstitious New England fans were alarmed by what uncharacteristic thing head coach Bill Belichick did at Super Bowl XLII (42) in Arizona?
  a) He was effusive in his pregame comments to the media
  b) He had been "trash talking" about Eli Manning before the game
  c) He was wore a sports coat instead of his usual grey sweatshirt during the game
  d) He wore a bright red sweatshirt during the game

QUESTION 163: What college did quarterback Steve Grogan attend?
  a) Abilene Christian
  b) Indiana State
  c) Kansas State
  d) Ohio State

QUESTION 164: The NFL named a new rule after Bill Belichick in 2008. What does the "Bill Belichick Rule" provide?

a) Home teams can videotape the opposition's pregame warm-ups
b) A defensive player can have a radio device in his helmet
c) It eliminated the existing dress code for coaches
d) If one team is ahead by 50 points they must go for first downs on fourth down situations, not kick field goals or punt the ball

QUESTION 165: What Patriots player was nicknamed "Sardines" after it was learned that his lucky charm was a can of sardines that he kept in his locker?
a) Otis Smith
b) Ron Sellers
c) Sam Adams
d) Sam Cunningham

QUESTION 166: Which of the following venues where the Patriots have played in the Super Bowl was an entirely open-air venue?
a) ALLTEL Stadium
b) Louisiana Superdome
c) Reliant Stadium
d) University of Phoenix Stadium

QUESTION 167: Which Patriots Super Bowl marked the first time the game was decided on the final play?
a) XLII (42)
b) XXXIX (39)
c) XXXVIII (38)
d) XXXVI (36)

QUESTION 168: The 1960 Patriots were a team made up mostly of ex-NFL veterans, former Canadian Football League players, semipro walk-ons, or players who had been cut from NFL teams in seasons past. However, the Patriots also selected 51 players from the first AFL college draft. How many of the players chosen in the college draft made the 1960 Patriots roster?

a) 1
b) 4
c) 8
d) 12

QUESTION 169: Since 1960 the Patriots have had 77 players on the roster who were products of New England Colleges. Boston College leads the pack with 27 players. Which NE school is next with nine former players suiting up as Patriots?

a) Boston University
b) University of New Hampshire
c) College of the Holy Cross
d) University of Massachusetts

QUESTION 170: Chuck Shonta was one of 26 offensive, defensive and special teams players named to the Patriots 1960s All-Decade Team. What position did he play?

a) Corner back
b) Outside linebacker
c) Punter
d) Running back

QUESTION 171: "Harpo" was the nickname for which Patriots Player?

a) John Hanna
b) Tim Fox
c) Bob Gladieux
d) Mosi Tatupu

QUESTION 172: "98.5 The Sports Hub" is the name of the flagship radio station of the New England Patriots radio network. What are the call letters for the station?

a) WBZ-FM
b) WBCN-FM

c)   WROR-FM
d)   WPAT-FM

QUESTION 173: What is the name of the official newspaper of the New England Patriots?
a)   New England Football Journal
b)   The Patriots Press
c)   Patriots Football Weekly
d)   Totally Patriots

QUESTION 174: Billy Sullivan, founder of the Patriots, also worked as an executive for another local team. Which sports team did he once work for?
a)   Boston Braves, baseball
b)   Boston College, basketball
c)   Boston University, hockey
d)   Boston Bruins, hockey

QUESTION 175: The one day record for the purchase of Patriots season tickets occurred on February 26, 1994—the day after Bob Kraft purchased the team from James Orthwein. To the nearest round number, how many tickets were sold?
a)   1,000
b)   3,500
c)   6,000
d)   10,500

QUESTION 176: Which year was Tom Brady named *Sports Illustrated's* Sportsman of the Year?
a)   2001
b)   2005
c)   2007
d)   2008

QUESTION 177: Which quarterback was *not* named to one of the Patriots All-Decades teams?

a) Drew Bledsoe
b) Steve Grogan
c) Babe Parilli
d) Jim Plunkett

QUESTION 178: The official Patriots 50th Anniversary team honored Gino Cappelletti as one of the team's captains along with which other Patriots great?
a) Tom Brady
b) Nick Buoniconti
c) Tedy Bruschi
d) John Hannah

QUESTION 179: Patriots founder Billy Sullivan was among the first NFL executives to offer naming rights to a stadium. How much did the Schaefer Brewing Company pay to have its name on the new stadium in Foxboro in 1971?
a) $1 million
b) $2.5 million
c) $3 million
d) $6 million

QUESTION 180: Businessman James Orthwein bought the Patriots in May of 1992 and wanted to move them to St. Louis, Missouri. What was he going to call the team if they relocated there?
a) St. Louis Bluesmen
b) St. Louis Gamblers
c) St. Louis Pioneers
d) St Louis Stallions

QUESTION 181: Which of the following Patriots players played for 16 consecutive seasons?
a) Julius Adams
b) Bruce Armstrong
c) Tedy Bruschi
d) Steve Grogan

QUESTION 182: Which player appeared in a record 212 games for the Patriots?
- a) Julius Adams
- b) Bruce Armstrong
- c) Tedy Bruschi
- d) Steve Grogan

QUESTION 183: The Patriots organization underwent a number of significant changes in 1993 that would lead to their great successes during the next decade. Which of the following did *not* happen that year?
- a) Adopted a new logo
- b) Changed uniform colors
- c) Drafted Drew Bledsoe
- d) Hired Bill Belichick

QUESTION 184: On April 16, 2005, Quarterback Tom Brady:
- a) Became a father
- b) Hosted *Saturday Night Live*
- c) Married super-model Gisele Bundchen
- d) Paid $2 million dollars in income taxes

QUESTION 185: In 2010, BenJarvus Green-Ellis became the first Patriots player to gain over 1,000 yards in a season since what other player?
- a) Cory Edwards
- b) Cory Dillon
- c) Curtis Martin
- d) Antowain Smith

QUESTION 186: The Patriots have had many players with the same last names over the years. Which name has appeared on the Patriots roster the most (13 times)?
- a) Brown
- b) Jones
- c) Smith
- d) Williams

QUESTION 187: What is the name of the book that Bill Belichick's father, Steve Belichick, wrote while he was a coach at the US Naval Academy and that many credit as an important influence on the younger Belichick?

    a) *A View from The Booth*
    b) *Education Of A Coach*
    c) *Football's Greatest Coaches*
    d) *Football Scouting Methods*

QUESTION 188: On October 4, 2010, the Patriots became the first NFL team to score a touchdown five different ways in the same game. They scored TDs by rushing, passing, returning a kickoff, returning a blocked field goal, and by an interception. Against which team did they accomplish this?

    a) Buffalo Bills
    b) New York Jets
    c) Miami Dolphins
    d) Pittsburgh Steelers

QUESTION 189: Which Patriots receiver played both ways during the 2004 season making 17 receptions and a touchdown as a wide receiver, and three interceptions as a defensive back?

    a) Deion Branch
    b) Troy Brown
    c) Patrick Pass
    d) David Patten

QUESTION 190: What 1980s era Patriots running back was called "The Blade" for his ability to cut down defenders with his great blocking ability?

    a) Tony Collins
    b) Craig James
    c) Andy Johnson
    d) Mark van Eeghen

QUESTION 191: After coaching the Patriots form 1997 to 1999 Pete Carroll became the Head Coach at which California University?
   a) UCLA
   b) USC
   c) UCAL
   d) Stanford

QUESTION 192: In the 1997 Divisional Playoff against the Steelers at Foxboro Stadium, what was the weather condition that made play difficult?
   a) Torrential rain then sleet
   b) Blinding snow
   c) Heavy fog
   d) Gale force winds

QUESTION 193: Who is the Patriots "Fan of the Year Award" named after?
   a) Lou Assad
   b) Joseph Mastrangelo
   c) Kathleen Sullivan Alioto
   d) Wilho W. Wauhkonan

QUESTION 194: Which Patriots defender has the most sacks to his credit?
   a) Julius Adams
   b) Richard Seymour
   c) Andre Tippett
   d) Ty Warren

QUESTION 195: Who holds the record for the most rushing yards in a single season for the Patriots prior to the AFL-NFL merger?
   a) Alan Miller—1960
   b) Ron Burton—1962
   c) Larry Garron—1964
   d) Jim Nance—1966

QUESTION **196:** *Sports Illustrated* magazine featured the Patriots on the cover five times in one year. What year was it?
   a) 2001
   b) 2004
   c) 2005
   d) 2007

QUESTION **197:** What opposing player said "Get Your Popcorn Ready" in some pre-game hype implying that he was going to put on a show against the Pats in 2007? (The Patriots won the game 48-27!)
   a) Champ Bailey
   b) Keyshawn Johnson
   c) Chad Ochocinco (Johnson)
   d) Terrell Owens

QUESTION **198:** What Patriots quarterback had a bit part in the movie *Airport 1975* starring Charlton Heston, Karen Black, and George Kennedy?
   a) Jim Plunkett
   b) Doug Flutie
   c) Vinny Testaverde
   d) Joe Kapp

QUESTION **199:** Which Patriots tight end set an NFL record for most touchdown receptions by a rookie (ten) in a single season?
   a) Russ Francis
   b) Benjamin Watson
   c) Rob Gronkowski
   d) Alge Crumpler

QUESTION **200:** Which Patriot was the first NFL player ever to run, catch, and throw for touchdowns in a single game since Walter Payton of the Bears did it in 1979?
   a) Tom Brady
   b) Troy Brown

c) David Patten
d) Jerome Wiggins

OVERTIME ANSWER KEY

___ QUESTION 161: A   ___ QUESTION 181: D
___ QUESTION 162: D   ___ QUESTION 182: B
___ QUESTION 163: C   ___ QUESTION 183: D
___ QUESTION 164: B   ___ QUESTION 184: B
___ QUESTION 165: C   ___ QUESTION 185: B
___ QUESTION 166: A   ___ QUESTION 186: D
___ QUESTION 167: D   ___ QUESTION 187: D
___ QUESTION 168: B*   ___ QUESTION 188: C
___ QUESTION 169: C   ___ QUESTION 189: B
___ QUESTION 170: A   ___ QUESTION 190: A
___ QUESTION 171: C   ___ QUESTION 191: B
___ QUESTION 172: A   ___ QUESTION 192: C
___ QUESTION 173: C   ___ QUESTION 193: B
___ QUESTION 174: A   ___ QUESTION 194: C
___ QUESTION 175: C   ___ QUESTION 195: D
___ QUESTION 176: B   ___ QUESTION 196: D
___ QUESTION 177: D   ___ QUESTION 197: D
___ QUESTION 178: C   ___ QUESTION 198: A
___ QUESTION 179: A   ___ QUESTION 199: C
___ QUESTION 180: D   ___ QUESTION 200: C

KEEP A RUNNING TALLY OF YOUR CORRECT ANSWERS!

Number correct: ___ / 40

Overall correct: ___ / 200

NOTES

#168—Patriots 1960 college draft choices on the roster: Ron
Burton, Northwestern (#1); Jim Davis, Oklahoma;
Harvey White, Clemson; Jack Rudolph, Georgia Tech.

New England Patriots IQ

It's time to find out your Patriots IQ. Add your total from all five chapters and see how you did! Here's how it breaks down:

GENIUS PATRIOTS IQ EXCEEDS BILL BELICHICK = 190-200
GENIUS PATRIOTS IQ DESTINED TO BE A FIRST BALLOT HALL OF FAMER = 180-189
GENIUS PATRIOTS IQ IS WORTHY OF A SUPER BOWL TITLE = 170-179
SUPERIOR PATRIOTS IQ IS WORTHY OF LEGENDARY STATUS = 160-169
SUPERIOR PATRIOTS IQ MAKES YOU ONE OF THE ALL-TIME GREATS = 150-159
OUTSTANDING PATRIOTS IQ PLACES YOU AMONG THE TOP PLAYERS = 140-149
ABOVE AVERAGE PATRIOTS IQ THAT EARNS YOU A NICE PAYCHECK = 130-139
SOLID PATRIOTS IQ THAT LETS YOU PLAY BALL FOR A LIVING = 120-129
AVERAGE PATRIOTS IQ LETS YOU WATCH ON THE BIG SCREEN TV = 000-119

About the Author

CHARLES "CHUCK" BURGESS has enjoyed an eclectic array of career experiences including being a carpenter, an army reserve officer, a radio host and producer, a writer, an educational consultant, a teacher, a coach, and a school administrator. In addition to his writing, Chuck is a managing partner of Edendale Entertainment, LLC, providers of literary, audio, and audiovisual properties featuring **Gramma's Critters** children's picture book and read along CD.

Born in Newton, Massachusetts, Chuck has lived in Greater Boston all his life. He is a graduate of Northeastern University where he was a member of the freshman and varsity football teams.

His first published article, "A Hammer and Saw Sled" appeared in <u>Popular Mechanics</u> magazine in 1970. Since that time he has written numerous sports and entertainment stories and his diverse work has appeared in newspapers and periodicals in both the United States and in Great Britain.

Chuck, a member of the Golf Writer's Association of America, published his first release for Rounder Books in 2005. **Golf Links** is the story of the pioneering working-class Scottish golf professionals who brought the game to America at the turn of the twentieth century, and their influence on the development of the game, including the discovery of America's first golf hero—Francis Ouimet.

Love that Dirty Water – The Standells and the improbable Red Sox Victory Anthem followed *Golf Links* and was Chuck's first co-authored project where he partnered with prolific baseball writer Bill Nowiln in 2007.

Chuck also co-authored **A View From the Booth** with former Boston Herald columnist Jim Baker. *A View From The Booth*, released in 2008, is a fascinating look at professional sports broadcasting, the New England Patriots, and the storied careers of legendary Patriots radio announcers Gil Santos and Gino Cappelletti.

Also by Chuck Burgess:

"A Scotsman's Journey To America" <u>Through The Green Magazine</u>, (Scotland) 2001.

"Alex Findlay: The Father of American Golf" <u>The Little Black Book of Golf</u>, Vol. 19.

"America's Forgotten Champion" <u>The Little Black Book of Golf</u>, Vol. 24.

"Cape Cod Celebration" <u>The Bulletin</u>, (Golf Collectors Society) 2002.

"Fix Your Grip..." <u>Pub Links Golfer Magazine</u>, 2002.

"Dirty Water" <u>Red Sox Annual</u>, 2007 (co-authored with Bill Nowlin).

"Golf Roots" <u>The Little Black Book of Golf</u>, Vol. 22.

"'Greatest Game' way off course" <u>Baltimore Sun</u>, 2005.

"Home On The Range" <u>The Little Black Book of Golf</u>, Vol. 20.

"Montrose Links to Birth of Golf in States" <u>Montrose Review</u>, (Scotland) 2002.

References / Acknowledgements

IN ADDITION TO my own recollections as a Patriots fan, author, and as a long time Patriots season ticket holder, the material contained in this edition has been gathered from a variety of sources that include official NFL publications, media guides, press releases, player and New England Patriots staff interviews, and the accounts and recollections of various members of the media.

I enthusiastically recommend a visit to The Hall at Patriot Place, the official Patriots football museum and the home of the Patriots Hall of Fame. There is a wealth of educational information and entertaining exhibits there for Patriots fans and for fans of the game in general. I wish to extend my appreciation to Bryan Morry, executive director of The Hall and to the many helpful staff members I met during my visits to The Hall during the development of "New England Patriots IQ."

I also wish to acknowledge and thank my friends, family members, and colleagues who have shared their personal knowledge, insights and favorite stories with me over the years about the New England Patriots. Too numerous to mention here by name, many have been previously acknowledged as contributors to "A View From The Booth" co-written with former Boston Herald columnist Jim Baker.

Special thanks are extended to Gino Cappelletti, Gil Santos, Roger Homan, Marc Cappello, and the entire WBZ - FM Patriots radio broadcasting team for their continuing cooperation and to my friend Tom Doyle of WROR-FM for his great eye for details and suggestions.

I'd also be remiss if I didn't thank my sons Chuck and Greg, my daughter Cathy Ann and my brother John who offered many great thoughts and feedback. Thanks also to Jim Rankin for sharing his great vintage Patriots "bubble gum" cards— they brought to mind many great memories. Once again, appreciation is extended to my former co-author Bill Nowlin of Rounder Records and Books for recommending me to Black

Mesa Publishing. And finally, nothing I write or publish would be possible without the continuing support and great editing of my wife Catherine.

About Black Mesa

BLACK MESA IS a Florida-based publishing company that specializes in sports history and trivia books. Look for these popular titles in our trivia IQ series:

- *Mixed Martial Arts (Volumes I & II)*
- *Boston Red Sox (Volumes I & II)*
- *Tampa Bay Rays*
- *New York Yankees*
- *Atlanta Braves*
- *Milwaukee Brewers*
- *St.. Louis Cardinals (Volumes I & II)*
- *Major League Baseball*
- *Cincinnati Reds*
- *Texas Rangers*
- *Boston Celtics*
- *Florida Gators Football*
- *Georgia Bulldogs Football*
- *Texas Longhorns Football*
- *Oklahoma Sooners Football*
- *Texas A&M Aggies Football*
- *Buffalo Bills*

For information about special discounts for bulk purchases, please email:

black.mesa.publishing@gmail.com

www.blackmesabooks.com

Also in the Sports by the Numbers Series

- *Major League Baseball*
- *New York Yankees*
- *Boston Red Sox*
- *San Francisco Giants*
- *Texas Rangers*
- *University of Oklahoma Football*
- *University of Georgia Football*
- *Penn State University Football*
- *NASCAR*
- *Sacramento Kings*
- *Mixed Martial Arts*

The following is an excerpt from

Curse in the Rearview Mirror: Boston Red Sox IQ, Volume II

Bill Nowlin

Available from Black Mesa Publishing

First

There's the anticipation leading up to the game. Long gone are the days that it was easy to stroll up to the Fenway Park box office and put down your money to buy a ticket and then walk right in. It's still possible to get game of day tickets, every game, but you can't count on there being many and if you are two or more wanting to sit together, the difficulty increases. There's also the scalp-free zone where you can buy tickets at no more than list price, and very often less, just before the game. You can also decide to get scalped and maybe pay an arm and a leg, depending – of course – on the laws of supply and demand. And there are the ticket resellers like StubHub or Ace Tickets or the ones who had the great TV ad a couple of years ago, Hig's.

You get into the park – always a little bit of an extra rush even if you've been to hundreds of games – maybe watch some batting practice. Someone throws out the ceremonial first pitch, there's the National Anthem, and finally, the real first pitch.

First up are the visitors (it wasn't always that way in major-league history, but it's been that way for a long, long time). The home team gets to bat last.

You don't really want to be late. Real fans don't understand it when they're going with a friend, and he/she doesn't have the same urgency to get there. I liken it to going to a movie. Why would you want to come in 10 minutes into the film?

Imagine showing up in time for the top of the second inning on June 27, 2003. You would have missed seeing the Red Sox score 14 runs in the bottom of the first inning off the Marlines. The game was pretty much over before it began and the crowd was buzzing all game long ... but you would have missed it.

Imagine what you would have missed if you'd missed the first two batters in the 1917 game on June 23. You would have missed seeing Babe Ruth punch umpire Brick Owens and get thrown out the game, and seeing Ernie Shore come in and start his perfect game.

On May 18, 2002, if you'd missed just the first nine pitches of the game, you would have missed seeing Pedro Martinez strike out the side, setting down Seattle with three strikeouts.

Every game starts with a first inning. And a lot can happen in the first.

TOP OF THE FIRST

QUESTION 1: What player hit a home run for the Red Sox, and then attended his college graduation that same day?

QUESTION 2: Which one of the following played against the Red Sox, rather than for them?
  a) Aristotle
  b) Archimedes
  c) Beckett
  d) Dante
  e) Darwin
  f) Emerson
  g) Ulysses
  h) Albert Schweitzer

QUESTION 3: What player never hit a grand slam throughout his entire Red Sox career until his final season, when he hit four of them?
  a) Mike Greenwell
  b) Ted Williams
  c) Jackie Jensen
  d) Babe Ruth
  e) Manny Ramirez

QUESTION 4: What new record did Jonathan Papelbon set in 2010?

QUESTION 5: Who hit the one-hopper that was famously "stabbed by Foulke"?

QUESTION 6: Four of the 10 American Leaguers to hit two grand slams in the same game were Red Sox players. Which one of the following was not one of the four?
  a) Nomar Garciaparra
  b) Ted Williams
  c) Rudy York
  d) Jim Tabor
  e) Bill Mueller

QUESTION 7: Can you recall who was the winning pitcher of what was arguably the greatest game in Red Sox history? We're talking Game Four of the 2004 ALCS against the Yankees.
  a) Curtis Leskanic
  b) Keith Foulke
  c) Curt Schilling
  d) Mike Timlin
  e) Pedro Martinez

QUESTION 8: Which Red Sox player made the most errors in one World Series game?

QUESTION 9: Errors happen more often than one might think. What is the longest stretch of games in which the Red Sox played error-free baseball?

QUESTION 10: How did the Church of the Redemption unintentionally prevent 50 Red Sox games from being played at Fenway Park?

TOP OF THE FIRST ANSWER KEY

___ **QUESTION 1:** Harry Agganis – and he didn't have far to go. It was June 6, 1954. Harry hit a two-run home in the fifth inning, for the fifth and sixth runs in a 7-4 win over the Tigers, then went down the street and graduated from Boston University after the game.

___ **QUESTION 2:** If you guessed the guy with the first and last name, you're right. Schweitzer was a right fielder for the St. Louis Browns from 1908 to 1911, known by the nickname "Cheese". He figured in Smoky Joe Wood's July 29, 1911 no-hitter against the St. Louis Browns, batting third and going 0-for-3.The other names are reflected in the following Red Sox player names: Aristotle "Harry" Agganis, Arquimedez Pozo, Josh Beckett, Dante Bichette, Danny Darwin, Emerson Dickman, and Ulysses "Tony" Lupien. The Sox also fielded a Cicero, a coach named Euclides, a Godwin, and a couple of Bards.

___ **QUESTION 3:** Answer: Babe Ruth

___ **QUESTION 4:** His save of Beckett's 3-1 lead over the Indians on August 3 gave him 25 saves on the season, making him the first pitcher in major-league history to record 25 or more saves in each of his first five seasons in the big leagues.

___ **QUESTION 5:** Cardinals shortstop Edgar Renteria, grounding out 1-3 to end the 2004 World Series.

___ **QUESTION 6:** Answer: B – Ted Williams.

___ **QUESTION 7:** Don't panic – it was Curtis Leskanic.

___ **QUESTION 8:** In five chances, Bill Mueller made three errors in Game Two of the 2004 World Series, which the Red Sox won, 6-2, over the Cardinals. Mueller was 2-for-3 at the plate.

___ **QUESTION 9:** In 1987, the Red Sox played the first game of the season without committing an error. Adding this game to the final 10 games of the 1986 regular season, that was a stretch of 11 consecutive errorless games – longest in franchise history.

___ **QUESTION 10:** Because the park was less than 1,000 feet from Fenway Park, a local statute prohibited the Red Sox from playing at Fenway on Sundays. From April 28, 1929 through May 29, 1932, the team was 17-31 with two ties in games held at Braves Field.

KEEP A RUNNING TALLY OF YOUR CORRECT ANSWERS!

Number correct: __ / 10

Overall correct: __ / 10

BOTTOM OF THE FIRST

QUESTION 11: In terms of intentions, which Red Sox player once received four intentional walks in one game?

QUESTION 12: Which Red Sox player holds the American League record for most intentional walks in a season?

QUESTION 13: When Daisuke Matsuzaka singled in Game Three of the 2007 World Series, it was the first time a Red Sox pitcher had a hit in the World Series since ... who?

QUESTION 14: Roger Clemens pitched three no-hit innings to kick off the 1986 All-Star Game in Houston, and received the win. At the time, he was the only Red Sox pitcher to record an All-Star Game victory. Six had taken the loss: Lefty Grove, Tex Hughson, Frank Sullivan, Monbouquette, Radatz, Tiant, and Eckersley – which is a pretty good collection of pitchers. Can you name the three Red Sox pitchers who have won All-Star Games since Clemens?

QUESTION 15: What five-time 20-game winner was signed by the Red Sox, but only appeared in one game - and lost it?
   a) Matt Clement
   b) Tom Seaver
   c) Jim Palmer
   d) Tony Clark
   e) Jack Chesbro

QUESTION 16: Can you name an American League pitcher who once won 41 games in a season for New York but whose career Red Sox record was 0-1?
   a) Herb Pennock
   b) Red Ruffing
   c) Jack Chesbro
   d) Mike Torrez

QUESTION 17: Who was the last Red Sox player to wear #9 before Ted Williams?
- a) Gordie Hinkle
- b) Dusty Cooke
- c) Bobby Doerr
- d) Ben Chapman

QUESTION 18: Which uniform number has been worn by more different Red Sox players than any other number?

QUESTION 19: Name the Red Sox player who wore the highest number of anyone in team history.

QUESTION 20: What Red Sox player finished his playing career with the Washington Senators but later had his number retired by the Red Sox?

BOTTOM OF THE FIRST ANSWER KEY

___ **QUESTION 11:** Manny Ramirez on June 5, 2001.

___ **QUESTION 12:** Ted Williams, 33 (1957) – a record he shares with John Olerud (1993).

___ **QUESTION 13:** Bill Lee, in Game Seven of the 1975 Series.

___ **QUESTION 14:** Pedro Martinez – 1999; Josh Beckett – 2007; Jonathan Papelbon – 2009.

___ **QUESTION 15:** E – Jack Chebsro.

___ **QUESTION 16:** C – Chesbro was 41-12 in 1904 for New York, but 0-1 for the Red Sox in 1909.

___ **QUESTION 17:** Chapman. The four men listed each wore #9 before Ted, in the order listed.

___ **QUESTION 18:** #28 – worn by 58 different players or coaches in the years since 1931, when the Red Sox first wore numbers.

___ **QUESTION 19:** J. T. Snow wore #84 in 2006.

___ **QUESTION 20:** Johnny Pesky, who played for both the Tigers and then the Senators in 1954.

KEEP A RUNNING TALLY OF YOUR CORRECT ANSWERS!

Number correct: ___ / 10

Overall correct: ___ / 20

Made in the USA
Lexington, KY
16 November 2015